How Do We Worship?

MARK CHAVES

An Alban Institute Publication

Library of Congress Card Number 99-97190

ISBN 1-56699-224-9

TABLE OF CONTENTS

FOREWORD

Americans worship. That short sentence seems so self-evident we are tempted to yawn and move on. So what?

But we need to ponder those words before moving on to other topics, to open up the important realities they contain. Americans, the most highly educated, secularized, affluent, technologically advanced, pluralistic, market oriented, and autonomy-valuing people on earth, do what? They worship. As the Midwestern mound cultures and the Southwestern kivas of our Native American pre-history remind us, they always have. As our national history tells us again and again the freedom to worship has been at the heart of the American experiment–shaping, fueling, and guiding our unfolding. People came to America and still come here seeking the freedom to worship–or not to–as they choose. The Bill of Rights enshrines as our first right the freedom of Americans to worship without the interference of government (at the time of its writing a most radical idea quite unprecedented in the other countries of the world).

What's more, Americans still worship–a lot. Our land and cityscapes are covered with places of worship, many of them filled every week, often several times. Pollsters keep checking and continue to turn up evidence (quite unlike that found in other parts of the world) of a huge number of Americans (a majority) who worship (many of them on a monthly basis, more of them less regularly, but at least occasionally). Contrary to the predictions of many social scientists, historians, philosophers, and theologians who just two decades ago prepared with confidence for a more and more secular world in which religion faded to the margins as modernity marched relentlessly on, worship is still one of the major facts of American life.

Yet, despite its centrality to who we are as Americans, despite its longevity and vitality, worship has not received the attention it deserves. To be sure, clergy and other religious professionals are taught how to lead and plan for worship, and there are scholars who specialize in the historical, cultural, and theological dimensions of it. Occasionally, worship breaks into the media world, primarily in televised worship services or reporting about a special worship service, say the funeral of a leader, or an anniversary event of an historic congregation. But the reality, the shape, the character, the impact, the variety, the scope of worship–its real role in American life–gets very little attention.

How Do We Worship? seeks to change that. For the first time, we have solid statistical evidence about the nature of worship in our society as a whole. Professor Mark Chaves has given us a status report on the worship life of Americans. In these few pages we can see quite far into this fundamental dimension of American life. We are able to measure the size of this phenomenon and get many clues to its shape and character. Conventional wisdom about worship–"Americans won't sit still for service longer than an hour" or "the average sermon these days is 15 minutes"–takes a beating here. There are surprises about our worshiping lives on every page.

This untold story about the importance and reality of worship needs to be told widely. It merits pondering by all seeking to understand and shape our life as a people. This publication, however, will most likely fall into the hands of religious leaders, of pastors, organists, worship committee members, seminary professors, and denominational officials, the "converted" who already believe that worship is very important. For them, *How Do We Worship?* provides a picture in which to place themselves, a map in which to find themselves. Through its information, analysis, case studies, and wonderful discussion questions it helps people become aware of what they take for granted, of what they do in this time when they focus on what Paul Tillich once called "ultimate concern." Careful attention to what is offered here makes possible comparisons and contrasts that will allow leaders and participants to discover what is special and distinctive in their own lives.

These pages also have the potential to release much needed conversations in our religious communities about very important issues surrounding and embedded within the worship of every congregation. America is the great worship smorgasbord–endless choices, endless competition. Increasingly, people come to any congregation, to any worship service, with a wide variety of preferences. Those who plan worship and who want to draw people into their communities of faith know just how powerful, how explosive the collision of those preferences can be.

The Alban Institute is honored to be able to make this important report available to you. We offer it as a "first fruit," a biblical term which implies that there is much more to come. The National Congregations Study upon which it is based has a great deal more to teach us about congregational life in America. We look forward to sharing some of those additional insights with you in the future. As a center for discovery and learning about congregational life we look forward to receiving reports from you about what you and your congregation learn as you review these findings. With you, we thank Professor Chaves for this important contribution to the life of our congregations and to the American experiment.

James P. Wind
President
The Alban Institute

ACKNOWLEDGMENTS

This report is the result of an uncommon three-way collaboration among practicing clergy, academic sociology, and a national center of expertise on American congregational life–the Alban Institute. Christopher Coble, a program officer in the religion division of Lilly Endowment Inc., encouraged us to seek meaningful clergy input as we moved forward on this report, and the Endowment provided the resources to make that input possible. As a result, clergy from around the country pored over preliminary results from the National Congregations Study (NCS), helped to identify the most interesting findings, and commented on drafts of the report along the way. If this booklet is at all compelling or useful to congregational leaders, it is in large measure thanks to Sue Berry, Jonathan Biatch, David Bird, Bruce Bowen, John Burciaga, Ken Carter, Martin Copenhaver, Wayne David, Kate Harvey, Paul Henneman, Alvin Jackson, Susan Johnson, Ron Lewinski, James Lewis, John McFadden, Duncan McIntosh, Lowell Schuetze, Nancy Sehested, Anne Stephens, and David Wood.

The Alban Institute is much more than the publisher of this little volume. James Wind and Leslie Buhler have been enthusiastic supporters of this project from its inception, and they established and managed the process resulting in this booklet. Alban senior consultants Terry Foland, Speed Leas, Alice Mann, Roy Oswald, Gil Rendle, and Ed White, like the clergy mentioned above, helped to separate wheat from chaff in the NCS results, and they read and commented on early versions of this manuscript. Two of the consultants, Gil Rendle and Speed Leas, have contributed congregational case studies to this booklet. Editor Beth Ann Gaede contributed more than mere copyediting. Whatever weaknesses remain are there only because I have been unable to incorporate all the insights and suggestions generated by this process.

Data collection for the National Congregations Study was supported by a major grant from Lilly Endowment Inc., and by supplemental grants from Smith Richardson Foundation, Inc., The Louisville Institute, The Nonprofit Sector Research Fund of The Aspen Institute, and The Henry Luce Foundation, Inc. None of these funders bear any responsibility for the contents of this report.

Deepest thanks go to the many congregations who participated in the National Congregations Study. This volume is dedicated to them.

Worship is the most central and public activity engaged in by American religious congregations. Ample portions of congregations' physical plants are often dedicated to worship. Much staff and volunteer time is spent preparing for worship. Large numbers of people participate in and help to create worship services week after week, year after year. For many people, worship is their main, perhaps their only, contact with congregational life. For others, congregational worship is the primary context in which they listen to live music, sing, see drama or dance, hear speeches, or look at paintings or sculpture.

Worship, in other words, holds a prominent place in congregational life. Perhaps because of its prominence, people in congregations ask many questions about worship. At least three different kinds of questions are raised. First are questions about how worship in one's own congregation compares to worship in a congregation down the street or across town. We know what our worship looks like, but what does theirs look like? Are they doing it better than we are? Should we be doing it more like they are? What is an average worship service like, and is our worship above or below average?

A second type of question commonly asked about worship concerns the proper balance between the traditional and the innovative. How traditional or innovative should worship be? How much, if any, experimenting should we be doing? How much experimenting do we *want* to do? Do we have to change the way we worship in order to grow? What does traditional worship mean in our denomination, anyway? How much room for legitimate variation in worship is there within our denomination or religious tradition?

These are not abstract, theoretical questions. They arise whenever congregations face concrete decisions about worship. Should we invest in a new hymnal? Should we change the way we say traditional prayers? Should we introduce a new kind of music? Should we encourage people to applaud during worship? Should we change our main service to accommodate alternative worship styles? Should we initiate a new service that allows for the expression of those different styles? All of these questions connect to the broader issue of the proper balance between tradition and innovation.

Worship can be a source of consternation, confusion, and conflict in congregations. One reason for these difficulties is that subgroups within a congregation might have different ideas about the proper and desirable way to worship. A third category of questions often asked about worship concerns these conflicts among subgroups. How can we have one worship service that attracts the young while satisfying the traditional old guard? How can we pass our faith to another generation with different worship preferences? Should worship be changed when new people with new expectations come to a congregation? If so, how? How can we learn about the worship preferences of those whom we want to reach? Is it necessary to have different services for different groups of people?

Even when different worship preferences are not connected to well-defined subgroups within a congregation, conflict over worship can still be intense. Perhaps the clergy's expectations regarding worship are different from the laity's. Perhaps those responsible for the music have yet other expectations. How is it possible to satisfy both the person who *hates* a particular innovative aspect of worship enough to refuse to be part of a service that includes it and the person who *loves* that aspect of worship and will not attend a service that lacks it?

This report contains information and tools intended to help you and your congregation grapple with the many vexing questions that arise regarding worship. It will help you to see a range of worship options in use today, to compare worship in your own congregation with typical worship practices in your denomination and beyond, and to ponder the connections between your congregation's worship practices, on the one hand, and its social characteristics, on the other hand.

This report draws on data from the 1998 National Congregations Study (NCS). The study is a nationally representative survey of 1,236 congregations from across the religious spectrum. It included Jewish synagogues, Muslim mosques, and Hindu temples, as well as Christian churches.

A clergyperson or other leader was interviewed in each of the NCS congregations, and that person was asked a host of questions about his or her congregation's programming, social composition, and activities. The NCS's use of scientific sampling procedures and its achievement of an 80% response rate make it a valuable resource for learning about congregations at the turn of the 21st century. Never before have students of congregational life had access to such wide-ranging information collected from such a high-quality and comprehensive national sample of congregations. The appendix to this report gives more detail about the NCS.

This report makes use of one set of NCS questions—those about worship. Chapter 1 describes some basic facts about worship in American religion. Chapter 2 introduces a tool that will enable you to assess certain aspects of worship in your congregation. Chapters 3 and 4 use NCS data to analyze where different types of congregations fall along two dimensions of worship practice—ceremony and enthusiasm. In its essence, this report offers a way to compare systematically worship in your congregation with worship in congregations in your and other denominations, and it offers a way to compare systematically worship in your congregation with worship in congregations having similar and different social and organizational characteristics. Brief case studies of four congregations are included to illustrate several of the themes emphasized in this booklet, and discussion questions are sprinkled throughout the report.

Although the NCS contains data from congregations across the religious spectrum, the vast majority of the congregations in the sample are Christian churches. Consequently, the results and assessment tools contained in this report apply most directly to Christian worship. Though the details may differ among congregations, however, many of the underlying issues explored in this booklet—the tension between tradition and innovation, the balance of formality and spontaneity, the conflicting worship preferences of subgroups within a congregation—arise in religious congregations of every tradition. This wider applicability is reflected, albeit incompletely, by the description of a Reform Jewish synagogue in one of the four congregational case studies included in this report. I am under no illusion that providing this one case study makes this report fully ecumenical. Nor does this one case sufficiently reflect the plurality of religious traditions in American society. No publication of this size could do that. The Reform Jewish case is included only to illustrate that at least some of the worship issues explored in these pages are issues not just for Christian worship but for all those who endeavor to create and maintain collective expressions of connection to a transcendent realm, however that realm is conceived.

ONE

Basic Facts About Worship in American Religion

The National Congregations Study gathered information about worship by asking how many of 29 different features a congregation's worship contains. Table 1 lists these features, the percentage of religious service attenders who experience each feature at worship, and the percentage of congregations having services containing each feature. We can think of these as the "elements" of worship. Very few, if any, actual worship services contain all 29 of these elements, but virtually all services in virtually all religious traditions contain some of them.

In a sense, worship services are constructed by choosing a subset of these elements and putting them together into a coherent whole. Sometimes the choice about how to construct a specific worship event from these elements is strongly influenced by denominational or congregational tradition. Sometimes a clergyperson or worship committee will consciously introduce new elements or remove elements that have long been included in a congregation's worship. Whatever the process by which worship services are constructed in different places, the basic idea is that real-life worship services are composed of subsets of these 29 elements.

The worship elements in table 1 are ranked from the most to the least common. Two of these elements–singing by the congregation and a sermon or speech–are essentially universal. No other element (except using a musical instrument of any sort, something closely associated with congregational singing) turned up in more than 80% of services, but virtually all services have both a speech and collective singing. Whatever else happens at worship services, worship in the United States means getting people together to sing and listen to somebody talk. Indeed, this combination almost completely distinguishes worship events from other

Table 1

What Happens at Worship?

	Percent of Attenders at Worship Services with:	Percent of Congregations whose Services have:
Singing by congregation	98	96
Sermon/speech	97	95
Musical instrument of any sort	90	83
People greet each other	84	79
Written program	84	71
Silent prayer/meditation	81	74
People speak/read/recite together	75	63
Laughter	74	73
Singing by choir	72	52
*People testify/speak about religious experience	72	78
*Skit or play performed by teens or adults	70	61
Organ	69	51
Piano	67	69
Applause	58	55
People call out "amen"	53	63
Singing by soloist	50	40
*Performance by paid singers or other performers	51	35
Something specifically directed at children	48	47
People other than leader raise hands in praise	48	45
Communion	48	29
Teens speak/read/perform	46	40
*People told of opportunities for political activity	36	26
Electric guitar	29	20
*Dance performance by teens or adults	29	17
Drums	24	19
*People speak in tongues	19	24
Visual projection equipment	15	12
Adults jump/shout/dance spontaneously	13	19
Incense	7	4

An asterisk (*) indicates the percent of congregations having a service with that feature at any time within the past year. For other elements, the percentage indicates the percent of congregations whose most recent main service included that element.

sorts of collective events in American society. On the one hand, few secular collective events–perhaps some birthday parties and some political rallies–routinely contain both singing and speech-making. On the other hand, only a few religious services–Muslim worship is less likely to involve singing and Buddhist worship is less likely to incorporate a speech–lack one or the other of these elements. Empirically, producing worship in the United States means getting people together to sing and listen to somebody talk. Beyond the explicitly religious aspects of worship services, then, these events occupy a very distinctive niche in American collective life. There are few places one can go, other than to a religious congregation's worship service, to sing and hear a speech.

There is another sense in which music and preaching are central to American worship. Not only do virtually all worship services, whatever the religious tradition, contain both congregational singing and preaching, but more than half (about 60%) of all the *time* spent in worship is taken up either with sermonizing or with music of some sort. The worship service experienced by the average attender lasts 70 minutes, and it contains a 20-minute sermon and 20 minutes of music. Put another way, the average worship service is about one-third listening to the leader talk, about one-third listening to or making music, and about one-third other kinds of activities, such as keeping silent, listening to someone read a text, or reciting something together.

The Importance of Congregational Size

Before examining how common some of the other worship elements are, it is necessary to focus for a moment on the issue of congregational size. The NCS reveals an important fact about American congregational religion: Although most congregations are small, most people are in large congregations. There are, of course, various ways to define congregational "participants" or "members." The NCS measured congregational size in three ways: (1) the total number of adults and children associated in any way with the religious life of the congregation, (2) the total number of adults and children who regularly participate in the religious life of the congregation, and (3) the total number of adults who regularly participate in the religious life of the congregation. Using the second of these measures, the NCS finds that 59% of U.S. congregations have fewer than

100 regular participants. The median congregation–the one that would be in the middle if we lined up congregations from the smallest to the largest–has only 75 regular participants. If we ask how many people attended the most recent main worship service rather than how many regular participants the congregation has, essentially the same picture emerges. Approximately 70 people attended the most recent main worship service at the median congregation.

Even if we use the most inclusive NCS size measure–the number of persons associated in any way with the religious life of the congregation–the large number of small congregations still is apparent: 36% of congregations have fewer than 100 people associated in any way with the religious life of the congregation. Perhaps most striking, 71% of U.S. congregations have fewer than 100 regularly participating adults.

Even though the median congregation has only 75 regular participants, the median *person* is in a congregation with 400 regular participants. To say this another way, the small congregation may be the typical congregation, but the typical attender of religious services is attached to a large congregation. To come at this point from another direction, consider that only 10% of American congregations have more than 350 regular participants, but those congregations contain almost half the religious service attenders in the country.

Figure 1 displays graphically these two aspects of the congregational size distribution. The vertical axis represents the cumulative percentage of persons who attend religious services, ordering them from those who attend the smallest congregations to those who attend the largest congregations. The horizontal axis represents the cumulative percentage of congregations, ordering them from the smallest to the largest congregations. The dashed diagonal line shows what would obtain if all congregations were the same size–if 10% of the people were in 10% of the congregations, 50% of the people were in 50% of the congregations, and so on. The concave curve illustrates the actual distribution of people across congregations. The curve shows, for example, that if we lined up congregations from the smallest to the largest and counted off half of all congregations, these smaller congregations would have only 11% of religious service attenders in them. The area between the curved line and the diagonal represents the basic point about congregations and size: most congregations are small, but most people are associated with medium to large congregations.

Figure 1
Distributing People Across Congregations

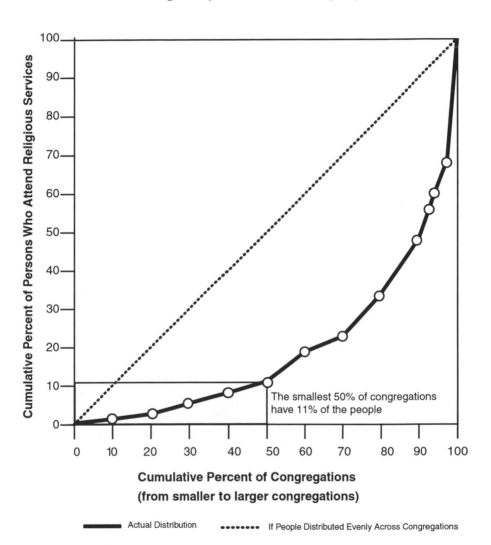

The smallest 50% of congregations
have 11% of the people

Cumulative Percent of Congregations
(from smaller to larger congregations)

━━━ Actual Distribution   ••••••• If People Distributed Evenly Across Congregations

This feature of congregations' size distribution leads us to ask two kinds of questions about worship practices. On the one hand, we might want to know about the typical worship practice of an average congregation. On the other hand, we might want to know about the typical worship experience of an average attender of religious services. If congregational size were not so skewed, these would amount to the same thing. But congregational size distribution is skewed, so what happens in the typical congregation is not necessarily the same as what the typical service attender experiences.

Looking again at table 1, for example, note that 69% of religious service attenders experience worship at which an organ is played, but worship at only 51% of congregations includes an organ. Keeping in mind the size distribution of people across congregations–especially the basic fact that most congregations are small but most people are in large congregations–the difference between these two numbers has a clear meaning: larger congregations are more likely than smaller congregations to have organ music. Put another way, the 51% of congregations with organ music at worship have 69% of the people in them.

For most of the worship elements listed in table 1, the numbers in the two columns are either about the same–meaning that large and small congregations are about equally likely to include that element in their worship–or, as with organ music, the number in the first column is bigger than the number in the second column. Large and small congregations, for example, are about equally likely to have singing by the congregation, a sermon, laughter, piano music, or applause. Besides organ music, larger congregations are more likely than smaller congregations to have singing by a choir or performances by paid singers. Having more people, it seems, presents a congregation with more human and financial resources to use in worship.

Only a few worship elements are more common in smaller congregations than in larger ones. People call out "amen" in 63% of worship services, but those worship services are attended by only 53% of the people. There is spontaneous jumping, shouting, or dancing at 19% of services, but only 13% of those who attend religious services experience worship of this sort. If larger size and the resources that come with it makes some ritual activities easier to accomplish, it may also make certain more informal elements more difficult to include in worship. I will return in chapter 4 to this relationship between congregational size and worship practice.

Readers should bear in mind that most of the numbers in table 1 are based on descriptions of a congregation's main worship service. In the case of congregations with multiple services, respondents decided for themselves which was the "main" service, and the NCS gathered data about that service. About one-quarter of American congregations have only one service in a typical week. Another quarter have two services, and the remaining half of congregations have three or more. If additional services have a character different from the main service, it could be that some of the elements occur in more worship services than indicated in table 1.

Two Dimensions of Worship

L ooking over the elements in table 1, it is clear that actual worship services are not random subsets of these elements. That is, some of these elements are more likely than others to occur together. You might be able to find a service, for example, that includes silent prayer, communion, speaking in tongues, and incense, but such a combination is more uncommon than a service with a sermon, organ music, and singing by a choir, or one with an electric guitar, speaking in tongues, and testifying. The process by which subsets of these elements are assembled to construct actual worship events is structured by a variety of factors, including denominational and congregational traditions, size (as we already have seen), and a congregation's social composition.

National Congregations Study data allow us to investigate some of these factors and ask what effect they have on congregational worship. To what extent is there an affinity between a congregation's worship style, on the one hand, and its ethnic, social class, or age composition, on the other? How similar or different are denominational traditions about worship styles? Are newer congregations characterized by distinctive styles? The rest of this report will explore questions like these.

Placing Your Congregation in Worship Space

NCS data provide an opportunity for you to assess how your own congregation's worship compares with worship in other congregations that are both similar to and different from your own. This report introduces two scales that will help in this assessment. One scale–the ceremony scale–

indicates the extent to which worship in your congregation contains elements that are more formal or ceremonial. The other–the enthusiasm scale–indicates the extent to which worship in your congregation contains elements that are more participative in an informal way. Note that these two scales are not opposites of each other–worship can be both highly ceremonial and highly enthusiastic. It also can be low on both ceremony and enthusiasm.

These scales–ceremony and enthusiasm–resonate with deep and long-standing issues regarding worship. The appropriate degree of enthusiasm, on the one hand, and formality, on the other hand, have been controversial issues in American religion at least since the Great Awakening of the 18th century. Debate over these issues continues today. How participative should worship be? How enthusiastic? How formal or informal? Although worship surely has dimensions other than the degree of ceremony or enthusiasm–a point to which I will return in the conclusion–this report focuses on these two dimensions because they tap aspects of worship rich with theological, historical, and practical meanings.

To use these scales, think of a *specific* worship service–perhaps your congregation's most recent main worship service–rather than "worship in general" or a "typical" worship service at your congregation. One interesting observation emerging from NCS data is that there often is no such thing as a "typical" worship service, even for a single congregation. Congregations have different types of worship events at different times of the year, and some may have different types of services, perhaps appealing to different groups of people, at different times of the day or week. For this reason, it is important to think of a specific worship service when using these scales. If you are in a congregation that has different types of services, it might be helpful to calculate two (or more) scores on each scale, one for a recent service of each type.

Figure 2 contains the scales. These scales have an empirical basis in that the nine specific elements included in each scale cluster together statistically. Because of this statistical clustering, the nine items in each scale together effectively represent the underlying dimensions of cere-mony and enthusiasm. This representation is not perfect (see box 1 for discussion of the limits of these scales), but they capture something meaningful about the degree of ceremony and the degree of enthusiasm in worship.

Figure 2
Ceremony and Enthusiasm Scales

Place a check next to each feature included in the worship service you are assessing.

	Ceremony Scale
Communion	_____
Organ music	_____
Silent prayer/meditation	_____
Part of the service specifically directed at children	_____
People speak/read/recite together	_____
Singing by a choir	_____
Singing by the congregation	_____
Sermon/speech	_____
Written program	_____

Total Ceremony Score (number of Ceremony items checked) _____

	Enthusiasm Scale
Adults jump/shout/dance spontaneously	_____
Applause	_____
Drums	_____
Electric guitar music	_____
People call out "amen"	_____
People other than the leader raise their hands in praise	_____
People speak in tongues	_____
People testify/speak about religious experience	_____
Piano music	_____

Total Enthusiasm Score (number of Enthusiasm items checked) _____

BOX 1

No Scale Is Perfect

This report focuses on two dimensions of worship—ceremony and enthusiasm—and it defines each of those dimensions in terms of nine elements that may be included in worship. These particular elements were selected because statistical analysis showed that they most effectively represent the underlying dimensions of ceremony and enthusiasm.

These dimensions, and the scales that define them, are tools intended to help us think about what happens in worship. They permit a valuable degree of concreteness. At the same time, readers should recognize their limits. These two dimensions identify basic and important aspects of worship, and the elements used to define them here are reasonable indicators of ceremony and enthusiasm in worship, but the items in these scales do not exhaust the meaning of ceremonial or enthusiastic worship.

It is easy to think, for example, of elements in addition to the eighteen used here that would indicate either ceremony or enthusiasm in worship. Whether or not the person leading the service wears a robe, or whether the sermon is delivered from a pulpit or the floor, for example, might be additional elements that could be added to the ceremony dimension. Spontaneous prayer, time for people to greet those around them, or people clapping their hands in time to music are elements that might be incorporated in worship to increase the level of enthusiasm.

Similarly, many of these eighteen worship elements might themselves be carried out with more or less ceremony and with more or less enthusiasm. For example, although "singing by the congregation" is on the ceremony scale because it indicates a certain kind of structured activity, congregational singing can be done with more or less enthusiasm. Although having a sermon or speech tends to indicate a certain degree of formality, sermons delivered conversationally, with some interchange between the leader and the people, will be experienced as less ceremonial and more spontaneous than sermons delivered without interaction between the speaker and the listeners. Because of the various ways the same elements might be carried out in different congregations, worship services with the same scores on these scales still might differ in their actual degree of ceremony or enthusiasm.

The point here is that although these scales each define ceremony and enthusiasm in terms of nine specific elements, there is no reason a congregation using these concepts to think about its own worship should be constrained by taking these scales too literally. These scales are intended to spark creative thinking about the ways in which your worship services embody ceremony and enthusiasm. If your congregation is looking for ways to raise or lower the level of ceremony or enthusiasm in worship, there is no reason to mechanically treat the elements used here as the only ways to influence these aspects of worship. Other elements beyond these eighteen might be relevant, and it might be possible to conduct the same element in a way that would make it express more or less ceremony or enthusiasm than it currently expresses.

Once you have a specific service in mind, simply go down each list of items in figure 2 and place a check next to each element that was included in that service, then count the checks in each column and write those numbers in the space indicated on figure 2. These are the ceremony and enthusiasm scores for your worship service. The basic idea is that worship with more of the ceremony (or enthusiasm) elements will tend to be worship that is experienced as more ceremonial (or enthusiastic).

Figure 3 contains the second part of this assessment tool. It is a grid defined by the ceremony and enthusiasm dimensions of worship. We can think of this grid as a "worship space" constituted by these two dimensions, much like geographical space is constituted by latitude and longitude. Any actual worship event can be located at a point in this space that corresponds to its scores on the ceremony and enthusiasm scales. The dotted vertical line gives the average score on the enthusiasm scale for worship services in the United States (3.9); the horizontal line gives the average score on the ceremony scale for American worship events (5.8). By placing an X on this grid at the point that corresponds to your own worship service's ceremony and enthusiasm scores, you can see at a glance how worship at your congregation compares on these dimensions with an average worship service across all congregations in the country.

Figure 3
A Two-Dimensional Worship Space

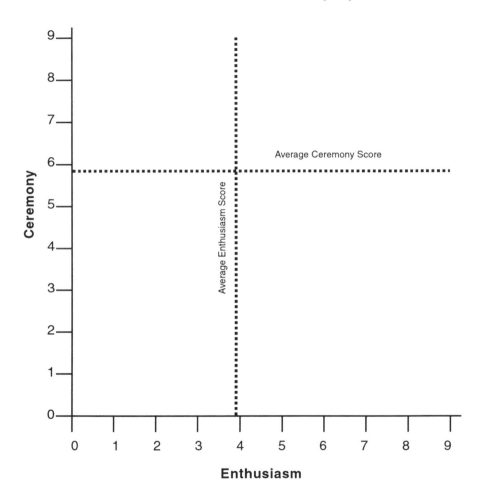

BOX 2

Other Ways to Use
the Ceremony and Enthusiasm Scales

What kind of worship do people in your congregation want? Do different subgroups want different sorts of experiences in worship? Although this report focuses on describing what actually happens in worship, it would also be possible and potentially informative to use the ceremony and enthusiasm scales to discover how people in your congregation would *prefer* worship to be. To do this assessment, have people go through each scale and check each item they would like to have included in worship—whether or not your worship service actually includes it. For example, perhaps a recent worship service included singing by the congregation, a sermon, a written program, and singing by a choir, for a score of four on the ceremony scale. But when asked what elements a person might want to have included in worship, perhaps someone would check singing by the congregation, a sermon, singing by the choir, silent prayer, and communion, for a score of five.

Asking a small group of people—perhaps a worship committee— to do this exercise can reveal differences in the preferred *levels* of ceremony and enthusiasm in worship, and it also can reveal different preferences that may exist regarding *aspects* of ceremony and enthusiasm. In the example described here, the hypothetical person in the paragraph above prefers worship slightly more ceremonial than what is the norm in this congregation, but he or she also would like to get to that level by incorporating silent prayer and communion rather than by using a written program. Beyond using these scales to describe your worship, using them to make visible people's preferences for worship style can generate additional insight and discussion about worship in your congregation.

These scales also might be used to help you assess your congregation's compatibility with another congregation with whom you are considering holding joint services. In a combined meeting of people from both congregations, ceremony and enthusiasm scores could be calculated twice—once for worship in each congregation. Then both the total scores and the specific elements that are checked could be compared. Although such a comparison certainly will not reveal all possible points of similarity and dissimilarity between two worship services, this sort of exercise might help to begin the conversation about those issues by making explicit some basic features of the worship that people in two different congregations are accustomed to experiencing.

THREE

Denominations in Worship Space

R eligious tradition, of course, is one of the main factors structuring what happens at worship. A randomly selected Roman Catholic worship service probably will differ from a randomly selected Assemblies of God worship service. A Presbyterian service will probably be different from a Baptist service, but the Presbyterian-Baptist difference probably will not be as large as the Catholic-Pentecostal difference. Figure 4 places selected denominations in the worship space defined by the ceremony and enthusiasm dimensions. It does this by using National Congregations Study data to calculate the average ceremony and enthusiasm scores for congregations in each denomination. Those averages constitute the center of each denomination's box in figure 4, much as the X you might have placed on figure 3 represents your own congregation's position in worship space. The center of each box is the denomination's center of gravity–where its average worship service falls.

The height of each box represents how much variation there is in ceremony among congregations within each denomination; the width of each box represents the variation in enthusiasm. The important point is that each box represents the region within the entire worship space that is occupied by each denomination. Denominations occupying similar regions in this space are placed together. Although more than 100 denominations are represented in the NCS, this map includes boxes only for denominations big enough to have at least nine congregations in the data set.

What does this mapping tell us? From one perspective, it tells us the "distance" between any two denominations' worship practice. These distances represent differences in the center of gravity among denominations. From another perspective, it allows us to assess the degree of overlap among denominations' worship. Denominations differ in their

Figure 4
Denominations in Worship Space

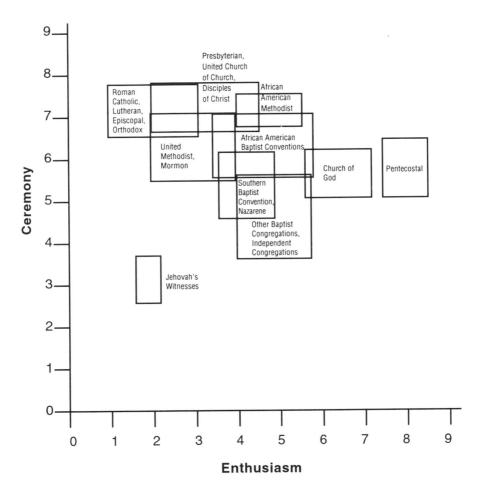

BOX 3

Do These Scales Apply
Only to Christian Worship?

Most of the elements in the ceremony and enthusiasm scales could be present in worship or ritual events within any religious tradition. Some elements, however, such as communion or speaking in tongues, are particular to Christian worship. The presence of these elements means it would not be appropriate to use exactly these scales to assess worship in other traditions. This is why, even though the NCS includes data on worship in synagogues, mosques, and Hindu temples, these groups are not pictured on figure 4.

Worship in these religious traditions can still be usefully analyzed in terms of enthusiasm and ceremony, however, though with scales composed of different elements. It is also likely that some of the social characteristics that influence Christian worship also influence worship in other religious traditions. Social divisions between the young and the old, innovators and traditionalists, newcomers and old-timers, rich and poor are present in every religious tradition, and it is likely that even in non-Christian congregations these divisions sometimes manifest themselves in conflict over how ceremonial or enthusiastic worship should be. (See case 3 for an example of worship conflict in a Jewish congregation.) Although these specific scales might not apply to non-Christian worship, the concepts they represent and the social and organizational characteristics to which they call attention probably apply more widely. With a bit of modification, these scales might be useful in discussions about worship even in non-Christian congregations.

---

center of gravity, but figure 4 reveals that there is considerable overlap in worship styles across denominations. From yet another perspective, this mapping can help you to see where your congregation's worship fits into the overall picture.

There are many interesting details to ponder in this map. In the upper-left corner of this space are Roman Catholic, Lutheran, Episcopalian, and Orthodox worship services. Worship in these traditions is on average the most ceremonial and least enthusiastic (as defined here) in the United States. Slightly to the right are the worship services of Presbyterian, United Church of Christ, and Disciples of Christ congregations. Worship in these congregations is just as ceremonial on average as worship in the more high church traditions, but it is on average slightly more enthusiastic, as measured by the NCS enthusiasm scale.

Note, however, that although the center of gravity of worship in these Reformed denominations is more enthusiastic than the center of gravity of worship in the more sacramental denominations, there is considerable overlap in worship styles across these denominations. That is, the Catholic congregations on the more enthusiastic side of Catholic worship are similar in this dimension to the congregations on the less enthusiastic side of Reformed worship. These traditions have different but overlapping worship practices.

Methodist worship, on average, is about as enthusiastic as Presbyterian worship, but it is a notch less ceremonial. Again, there is substantial overlap: the most ceremonial Methodist worship services are likely to be indistinguishable on this dimension from the more informal Presbyterian services. Worship in Southern Baptist congregations is both less ceremonial and more enthusiastic than Methodist worship, but note the variation among Baptists. Independent Baptist congregations have worship that is less ceremonial and more enthusiastic than Southern Baptist worship, implying that Southern Baptist worship is on average more like Methodist worship than is worship in independent Baptist congregations. Congregations with no denominational affiliation have worship styles much like independent Baptist congregations. Worship in the congregations associated with one of the several African American Baptist conventions overlaps considerably with Southern Baptist worship, but it lies a bit further along the enthusiasm scale. African American Methodist congregations, interestingly, are about as enthusiastic in their worship as African American Baptist congregations, but the African American Methodists are a notch more ceremonial in their worship.

Only two religious groups pictured here occupy worship space that does not overlap at all with another group. Pentecostal congregations have the most enthusiastic worship, and the variation in worship among these congregations is small enough that there is no overlap (as defined here) between their worship space and the next most enthusiastic group of congregations–those associated with the various Church of God

---

BOX 4

Discussion Questions for Figure 4

1. Is worship in your congregation very near the middle of the space occupied by your denomination, meaning that worship in your congregation is similar to the average type of worship for congregations in your denomination? Or is your worship more or less enthusiastic, more or less ceremonial, than the average worship service in your denomination? Why do you think your congregation falls where it does relative to other congregations in your denomination?
2. Is worship in your congregation more like worship in a denomination other than your own? If so, why might this be true?
3. When it comes to worship, are you concerned about your congregation's position compared to other congregations in your denomination? Would you like worship in your congregation to be more like average worship in your denomination? Would you like it to be less so?

---

denominations. Jehovah's Witnesses have worship services that are characterized by low levels of both ceremony and enthusiasm; their worship services are distinct in American religion in the extent to which they resemble classroom instruction sessions.

As mentioned above, placing your congregation's worship on this denominational map will illustrate where it falls in relation to worship in several religious traditions in the United States. This sort of analysis cannot tell you what worship in your congregation *ought* to be like, but perhaps it will help you to think about where your congregation is in relation to your own and other denominations, and perhaps it will help you to think about the directions–if any–in which worship in your congregation might move.

FOUR

Congregational Traits and Worship Space

D enomination is not the only factor shaping worship practices. Different ethnic groups sometimes carry distinctive worship styles, poor people may have different expectations for worship than the better-off, young people may want elements in worship that are different from those preferred by older people, and so on. A congregation's social composition, in other words, is likely to shape worship, whatever its denomination. Indeed, one important form of conflict within congregations occurs when the people in a congregation have expectations for worship that clash with what might be long-standing denominational worship traditions. National Congregations Study data can be used to explore how congregations with different social characteristics worship. These explorations, applied to your congregation, might help you to assess how your congregation's worship compares to the worship of congregations of similar social composition. Figures 5 through 9 display how congregations with different characteristics map onto worship space.

Race

Figure 5 compares congregations that have no African Americans with those that are 100% African American. (There are too few NCS congregations composed predominantly of Latinos or other ethnic groups to permit including them in this figure.) Congregations falling between these two extremes of racial composition fall in the region between the two boxes on this figure. The higher the percentage of African Americans in a congregation, on average, the closer that congregation tends to fall to the

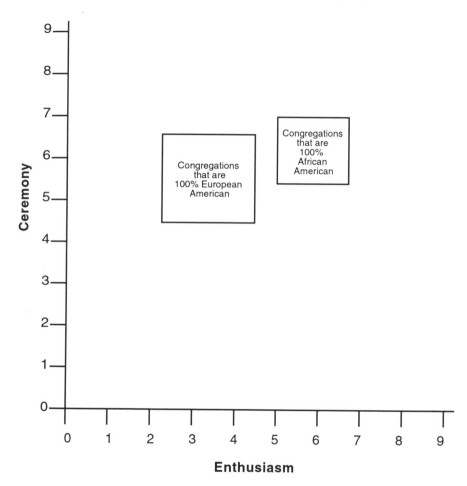

Figure 5
Racial Composition and Worship Space

right box in figure 5. Black congregations of whatever denomination have substantially more enthusiastic worship than do white congregations, although the two groups of congregations display similar degrees of ceremony in worship. Race seems to influence the degree of enthusiasm in worship more than it influences the degree of ceremony.

How might this picture, and the others to follow, be used to help think further about worship? Perhaps most important, by breaking worship services down into these two dimensions–ceremony and enthusiasm–and by further breaking down those dimensions into their nine constituent elements, we can think more precisely and perhaps more imaginatively about a congregation's worship practice and how it might be changed, if change is desired.

With respect to race, for example, figure 5 implies more than that African Americans are likely to engage in more enthusiastic worship than white Americans–something already well known. It says something more precise: African American worship services have on average between 5 and 7 of the elements composing the enthusiasm scale, and predominantly white congregations have on average only 2 to 4 of those elements. A congregation with worship that has only three elements from the enthusiasm scale, but in which, say, 40% to 50% of the people are African American, might ask whether the congregation might better meet people's expectations about worship by adding one or two elements from the enthusiasm scale. In this way, assessing where your congregation lies in this worship space and comparing it to where variously defined subsets of congregations lie can help you to think about worship options.

Age Composition

Figure 6 examines how worship varies as a congregation's age composition changes. The left box is the region occupied by congregations with fewer than 20% of adults under 35 years old; the right box is the region occupied by congregations with more than 40% of adults under 35 years old. Congregations falling between these two categories tend to fall in the area between these two boxes. Unlike the comparison between predominantly black and predominantly white congregations, there is noticeable overlap on both dimensions between average worship in congregations with the fewest and the most young adults. Still, the center of gravity differs for

CASE 1

Ethnic Change and Worship
in a Methodist Church

By Gil Rendle

Metropolitan United Methodist Church is a tall-steeple congregation located in the heart of a large city, next to the city hall and several skyscraper corporate centers that along with this church dominate the city's downtown.

Metropolitan Church was once large and the membership almost exclusively white. Historically, the members were largely middle-class and upper-middle-class and were highly appreciative of the traditional and classically oriented music and worship in this congregation. A former beloved and long-tenured pastor was widely known as an exceptional preacher. In more recent years, membership has shrunk to 300 people with an average worship attendance of about 150.

Over the past several decades the demographics of the city have changed considerably, becoming much more ethnically, racially, and nationally diverse. The church has found itself surrounded by corporate and city leaders during the day but an increasingly diverse and poor population in the evenings and on weekends. As a way of addressing the church's changing environment, a male and female clergy team was appointed to this congregation. Both pastors were white and spoke English only. With strong, sometimes confrontative, leadership, the team helped the church address the realities of its current situation and to begin to sense the opportunities for ministry that were present.

The new clergy team quickly began to expand and diversify the worship experience. Beginning with a formal worship service that followed the liturgical tradition of the denomination, they began to include traditions and forms of worship that reflected the con-gregation's multiracial, multinational neighbors. A second worship service was initiated that used African American and gospel worship and music forms. In both services preaching became less formal and academic, and more expository and conversational. The clergy often left the pulpit to preach, speaking either from the floor of the sanctuary or from a "preaching table" near the central altar. The white clergy team intentionally began to build a much more diverse music and ministry staff, with particular attention to the inclusion of African American leaders, and for a considerable period of time they hired a well-known African American pastor to preach on a regular schedule at the church.

Special services reflecting different ethnic constituencies within the congregation were regularly offered. Traditional European and African American worship forms were joined by Native American dance and storytelling, Dixieland jazz, Irish banjos and tin flutes, and an increasing array of new experiences as leaders could be found.

The congregation began to respond to the varieties of worship and the sharpening vision for diversity and inclusiveness in this church. The church was not growing dramatically, but the decline of membership had stopped, and the church was beginning to look like and respond to the city that surrounded it. When one of the pastors encountered on the street a homeless woman who worshipped with them, the woman proclaimed boldly, "I know you. You're from the church with the open arms." The name stuck, and the congregation became known as "the church with the open arms."

As the congregation was changing, so were the leaders. The white male co-pastor left for another ministry, the white female minister took up the position of senior pastor, and an African American male became full-time associate pastor. The composition of the lay leadership group also became increasingly diverse with regard to race, nationality, gender, and length of tenure.

These changes were not always smooth. Although there was strong support among the membership for the vision of the church, there were repeated arguments about the appropriate steps toward that vision and how those steps might affect the details of daily life in the church. Often the disagreements would bring movement to a halt. Equally unsettling was constant and wearing criticism directed at the clergy by lay leaders of the congregation.

Many of the arguments were about worship at the church. There was a high level of sensitivity to the leadership in the worship services: which service would get the African American music leader, which service would have the white and which the black preacher, what kind of music was to be sung, how formal should the greeters and ushers be, and how long should worship last? Should worship be over and done with in an hour, or should people be allowed to worship until they were done?

Eventually, congregational leaders, both clergy and lay, came to understand that diversity means that not everyone will agree with everyone else on all issues. They came to see that the conflicts that leaders routinely experienced with one another were not barriers to their vision. The disagreements were the result of their vision being accomplished and were to be managed rather than avoided or suppressed. If disagreements and competing preferences were built into their leadership circle because of the social diversity in that circle, leaders would have to learn ways of making decisions that would not require consensus. They would have to learn basic tools of conflict management. They would have to agree to follow basic guidelines or behavioral covenants about treating one another with respect while they were busy disagreeing with each other.

Discussion Questions

1. Is there racial or ethnic diversity in your congregation? If so, does it generate disagreement about what worship should be like? Why or why not?
2. If you had to choose between an ethnically and racially homogeneous congregation—one that therefore did not experience conflict about worship over those divisions, at least—and a racially or ethnically diverse congregation with associated conflicts over worship, which would you choose? Why?

congregations with different age structures. Congregations with more young people tend to have worship that is both more enthusiastic and less ceremonial than worship in congregations with fewer young people. It is important to emphasize that it is impossible to know the direction of the relationship between the presence of young people and worship style. Do congregations with more young people alter their worship practices in order to better match the preferences of their young constituents? Or do young people flock to congregations with slightly more enthusiastic and

Figure 6
Age Composition and Worship Space

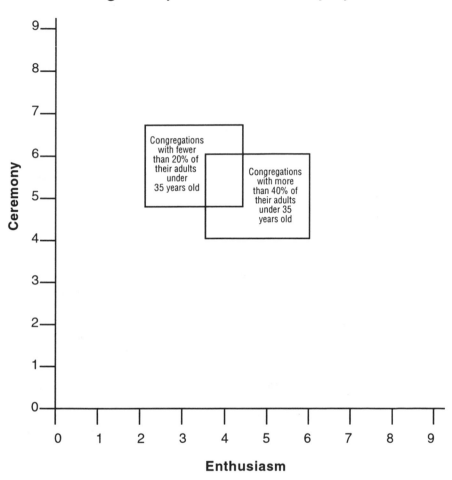

CASE 2

Intergenerational Worship Issues in a Baptist Church

By Gil Rendle

Grace Baptist Church is a tall-steeple church in the arts district of a small city in the northeast. It was once a large congregation that over a period of 40 years had shrunk to about one-third of its greatest size. Over the past four years, however, with a senior pastor who was a skilled leader and a notable preacher, the congregation had reversed its decline and had grown by over 20%. This was a substantial accomplishment for an urban church located in a setting where the city itself was struggling.

Much of the growth came from younger families with children who had been targeted by the senior pastor, staff, and lay leaders for invitation to this church. Some were drawn to the area because of the arts district, and many came out of appreciation for the urban setting of this congregation. A good number of the new members as well as the older members drive from other areas in the city and the surrounding suburban communities to participate in this congregation.

Almost 40% of the congregation have been members for 10 years or less. These shorter-tenured members tend to be younger and carry cultural values that are different from longer-tenured members. About half the members have been there for 20 years or more.

One of the strategies used at this church to include its new members was to form a children's choir for the growing number of children who came with their parents. Soon after the choir was formed, the children sang a special anthem in morning worship. There was overwhelming satisfaction in the congregation for what they were witnessing. They were pleased to see so many children. Members were delighted to have them included in worship, and they loved the children's singing.

The pleasure was disrupted immediately after the children finished singing, however, when a number of people in the congregation applauded. The applause and the response that it drew divided the congregation along generational and tenure lines.

The older generation and the longer-tenured members were adamant that applause in worship was inappropriate. Worship is a sacred event, they argued. It is a formal experience, and we dress and behave our best when we are here because we are in the presence of God. We do not applaud as if this were a performance.

The younger generation and shorter-tenured members replied by saying that they were not applauding a performance, they were participating with the children in worship. They spoke about their delight in having the children take part in worship. And they spoke about worship as a place to be with God "as you are," without having to be formal and act in ways that you would not act in other settings. Applause did not diminish worship for them. It offered them a way to be engaged and included in a deeper manner.

During a meeting with congregational leaders, one 40-year-old member who had been at this church for about 16 years captured the tension between the two generations by talking about what it felt like to "live in the middle." "My child is one of those kids up there in the choir who is singing. I need to say that I am going to applaud when they sing, because I want my child to feel appreciated, and I want her to feel like she has a place in this church. But I also need to say that when I am applauding, I know that I am breaking the heart of my father, who is sitting next to me in the pew."

Discussion Questions

1. In your congregation, are younger people and newer members more likely than older and longer-term members to advocate making worship more informal? If not, why not?
2. Whether or not applause occurs at worship in your congregation, do you think applause is more like responding to a performance or more like participating in an event? How does your answer to this question relate to your opinion about the appropriateness of applause at worship?
3. Are hard feelings unavoidable in a situation like this? Is someone's heart always broken when worship practices change? Why or why not?

CASE 3

Intergenerational Worship Issues in a Reform Synagogue

By Speed Leas

In a Reform Jewish congregation in the Midwest, older and younger members disagreed over what worship should be like. In the early days of the Reform Movement in North America, the practice was to move away from worship elements that differentiated Reform Jews from the larger (Christian) culture. Less Hebrew was used in the services of worship, many of the songs sounded like Protestant hymns, members of Reform congregations eschewed the wearing of the tallith (a shawl worn in worship) or a yarmulke (skullcap), and the prayer book was the Union Prayer Book, whose language was very similar to that of the King James Version of the Bible. All of this was true of this Midwestern congregation.

In recent years, younger members of this congregation have been asking for more Hebrew in the services and more music from Israel. They are wearing yarmulkes whenever they are at the synagogue as well as in worship, and talliths in the worship service. These practices have made many of the long-time members ill at ease. What the younger people want to do feels foreign to the older members. Not only have the older members grumbled about the practices of younger members, they have tried to legislate limits to the use of Hebrew in the sanctuary.

This congregation's worship committee was charged with exploring these issues. They collected more information from the members of the congregation about their preferences in worship, and they expanded the committee so that it better represented all the perspectives in the congregation. The committee then met for a full day and an evening to hash out the temple's policy (and the rabbi's and cantor's policy) on worship.

They decided that the Friday night service would contain a significant amount of Hebrew and would use a new, more Hebrew-centered prayer book. The main service on Saturday morning also would have a good deal of Hebrew. Each week on the sabbath, however, a third service would be held in a large chapel at the other end of the building from the main sanctuary. In this service, the older Union Prayer Book would be used.

The old-timers were still pretty grumpy after these decisions. Even though they were not able to continue worshiping the way they had been in their younger days, however, they knew they had participated in important decisions about the future of worship in their congregation.

Discussion Questions

1. Which party in the conflict described here was on the side of maintaining "tradition"? What does it mean for worship to be "traditional"?
2. In your congregation, how do you balance faithfulness to a worship tradition with responsiveness to change?
3. What are the pros and cons of establishing different worship services for people with different preferences?

slightly less ceremonial worship? The NCS cannot adjudicate between these two possibilities. It can only establish that there is a correlation between worship style and a congregation's age composition; it cannot tell us whether changes in worship style will help a congregation attract–or hold on to–more young adults. This caveat applies to all the relationships explored in this report. I emphasize the cause-effect ambiguity here, however, because the breadth and depth of concern in American religion about maintaining the loyalty of young adults makes it particularly important to sound a note of caution about what these patterns might mean.

Social Class

Figure 7 compares worship in congregations where fewer than 10% of the people are in households with 1998 incomes less than $25,000 to worship in congregations where more than 40% of people are in such low-income households. Interestingly, this figure looks much like the previous figure showing congregations' age composition. The region of worship space occupied by congregations with more low-income people is very similar to the region occupied by congregations with more younger people in them. The region of worship space occupied by congregations with fewer low-income people is very similar to the region occupied by congregations

Figure 7
Income Level and Worship Space

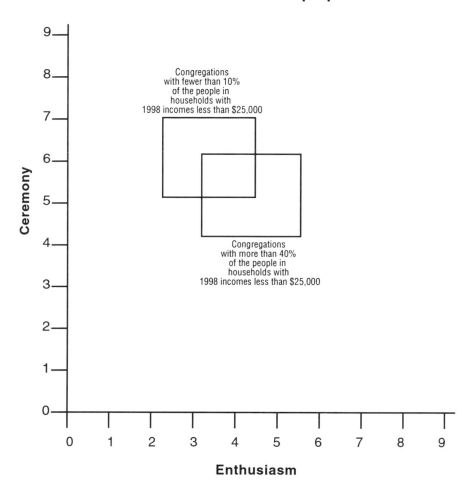

where the average age of the people is higher. If we lined up congregations from those with the richest people in them to those with the poorest people in them, we would find worship is more enthusiastic and less ceremonial as we move down that line.

The similarity between figures 6 and 7 raises another interpretive subtlety concerning the results reported in this booklet. Because younger adults on average have lower incomes than older adults, perhaps the relationship between age and worship depicted in figure 6 is really just a disguise for a deeper relationship between worship style and income level. That is, maybe income but not age is related to worship practice, and the pattern in figure 6 emerges only because younger adults on average are also lower-income adults. Alternatively, perhaps the relationship between income and worship depicted in figure 7 is produced merely by the fact that lower-income people also tend to be younger, and it is age rather than social class that is independently related to worship styles.

Fortunately, in contrast to the ambiguous causation described in the section on age composition, NCS data can tell us whether the relationship between age and worship is reducible to the relationship between income and worship. It is not. The relationship between age and worship depicted in figure 6 holds even after the correlation between income and age (among other things) is taken into account.

The relationship between income and worship is more complex, however. Additional analysis suggests that once age and other factors are controlled, congregations with more low-income people have worship that is less ceremonial but not significantly more enthusiastic. The income level of a congregation appears to be a more important influence on the degree of ceremony in worship than on the degree of enthusiasm.

Region

More generally, each of the relationships described in this report holds even when multiple other variables are statistically controlled. None of them is fully reducible to other congregational characteristics. A relationship that *is* reducible in some measure to other characteristics is that between region and worship style. New England congregations, for example, occupy a space near the upper left corner of the two-dimensional worship grid–higher and further left than the space occupied by congregations in any other region. Does this mean there is a distinctively New England worship style? More generally, are regional worship styles an important influence on worship? The answer appears to be yes and no.

Regional differences in ceremony largely disappear when de-nominational differences are taken into account, but regional differences in enthusiasm remain. New England congregations are rather high on ceremony, for example, because there are disproportionately more Catholic (and other denominations that worship in a high-ceremony, low-enthusiasm manner) congregations in this region than in other regions. The regional difference in the extent to which worship is high in ceremony appears to be reducible to denominational differences, which is why the regional relationships are not displayed in a figure; such a figure would be misleading. At the same time, however, there appear to be distinctive regional worship styles when it comes to enthusiasm. New England congregations, for example, display in their worship fewer elements indicating enthusiasm than do congregations in other regions, even after other variables are held constant.

Size

The relationship between size and congregational worship has already been touched on, but figure 8 adds something important to the above discussion. The top box shows the region of worship space occupied by congregations with more than 900 regularly participating adults; the bottom box shows the space occupied by congregations with 75 or fewer regularly participating adults. Interestingly, congregational size seems much more strongly related to the ceremony dimension of worship than to the enthusiasm dimension. It appears that the additional resources often available to larger congregations–more people to sing in choirs; more money to hire soloists, maintain an organ, or print a bulletin–have more significant consequences for worship than do the group dynamics that might make a service with 25 or 50 people different from a service with 500 or more people in attendance.

Although some worship elements (for example, inviting testimonies from the congregation) might be more difficult to include in large groups than in small ones, it appears that large size does not necessarily prevent incorporating at least some elements that make worship more enthusiastic

Figure 8
Size and Worship Space

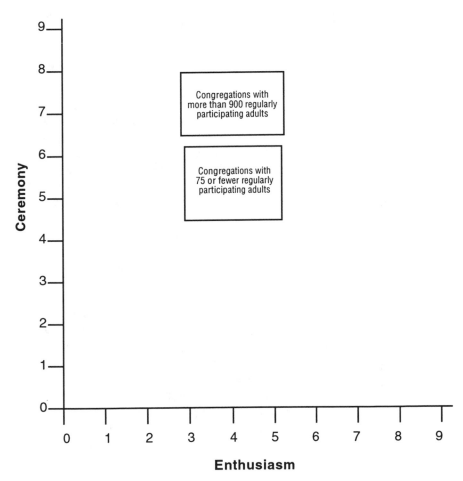

CASE 4

Growth and Worship at a Presbyterian Church

By Gil Rendle

Central Church was a traditional family church located in a suburban community near a large city in the South. Over the past thirty years the membership hovered between 400 and 500, with average worship attendance in the 200 to 250 range. Other congregations in the immediate area grew considerably during that same time period, matching the demographic growth in the surrounding communities. The outreach portion of the church's budget was substantial, but little or no personal involvement by members was encouraged. Worship used the same format most Sundays and was based on an old version of the Presbyterian Book of Order.

In 1993 the congregation called a young and dynamic pastor and proclaimed that they were ready to be led and energized to try new things. The first "new thing" they tried was calling a second pastor, a very capable woman. Although she was technically an associate pastor, the two clergy quickly formed a team ministry and were known and respected in the congregation as a collaborative team. Working with one another and the music leaders, the clergy team redesigned worship to be more interactive, which people received very favorably. The church also increased hands-on involvement, traveling to Mexico each year to build houses, participating in Habitat for Humanity projects, working in soup kitchens, volunteering for literacy programs, and similar activities. They established a unique monthly informal worship service led primarily by laity that included contemporary music, communion, and lay speakers.

The next years saw dramatic growth. In 1995-1996 membership increased almost 50%. Worship attendance increased by almost 100%, and the budget increased by 46%. Sunday School attendance increased almost 75%.

Growth brought a number of challenges regarding worship, among other things. The congregation was running out of space in their sanctuary. Maximum seating capacity was 340, and they regularly experienced attendance around 320 at the 11:00 A.M. service. The congregation ran out of Sunday School space and discovered that parking was an issue for many of their members. With such growth, it also was difficult to create in worship the sense of community and intimacy that was so important to the members. Congregational leaders wondered about the appropriate ways to use their clergy in multiple worship services and how growth might affect the allocation of staff time in other areas as well.

Options for this congregation's development included adding a third worship service, expanding the building, relocating, or starting a new congregation. After exploring these options through a long-range planning committee, congregational leaders decided to stay in their current facility, keep it at its present size, and initiate a third regular weekly worship service on Sunday morning. The new worship service was designed as an informal alternative that would include contemporary music, and have storytelling rather than preaching. Adding this service meant increasing support for the music leadership of the church, developing new agreements with the clergy team, and building commitment among members who would help lead, greet, and usher at the additional service.

Within a month after the initiation of the new third service, there were an additional 300 people worshiping at Central Church, increasing average attendance at Sunday morning worship by an additional 40%.

Discussion Questions

1. Do you think the changed worship practices caused this congregation's growth, or did the changed worship practices allow the congregation to respond to the community's growth? Do you think changing your congregation's worship practices would lead to growth? Why or why not?
2. When, if ever, should "contemporary" or "alternative" worship styles be resisted, even if they are popular? Are there worship practices you would not want your congregation to adopt, no matter how popular they might be with others? If so, what are they?
3. If your congregation has grown (or declined) in recent years, how has that change in size influenced worship?

and participative. In American religion, worship in the largest congregations is on average about as enthusiastic (as measured here) as is worship in the smallest congregations. Size, in and of itself, does not seem to be a barrier to the expression of enthusiasm in worship.

Founding Date

Figure 9 compares worship in the oldest congregations–those founded before 1877–with worship in the youngest–those founded since 1970. Here the focus is on the founding date of the congregation itself, not the age of the people in the congregation. The youngest congregations–those founded most recently–tend to have worship that is both more enthusiastic and less ceremonial than worship in the oldest congregations. If boxes representing congregations founded in the intervening years were placed on this chart, beginning with those founded first and moving toward those founded most recently, the boxes would start very near the upper left corner of the worship space and migrate steadily toward the lower right corner. It seems that over the last 100 years of American religious history, each successive wave of new congregations has adopted worship that is slightly more enthusiastic and slightly less ceremonial than the wave before it.

This is an intriguing pattern open to several interpretations. On the one hand, it could mean that over time there is a trend in American worship from the upper left part of the worship space to the lower right part–that American worship has become and continues to become less ceremonial and more enthusiastic as time goes on. Based on this interpretation, newer congregations have more enthusiastic and less ceremonial worship because they are part of a broader cultural movement toward less formal and more participative ritual, and they portend a future that continues to move in that direction. On the other hand, this pattern could mean that more enthusiastic and less ceremonial worship always, at every historical juncture, is found in the more recently founded congregations. Perhaps this style of worship characterizes younger congregations, not because there is a general trend in this direction, but because this sort of worship is more difficult to sustain over long periods of time in a single congregation. By this logic, congregations that start out with less ceremonial and more enthusiastic worship might become more ceremonial and less enthusiastic as they age and grow and become more bureaucratic and more staid. Either of these dynamics could produce the pattern in figure 9, and NCS data cannot

Figure 9
Founding Date and Worship Space

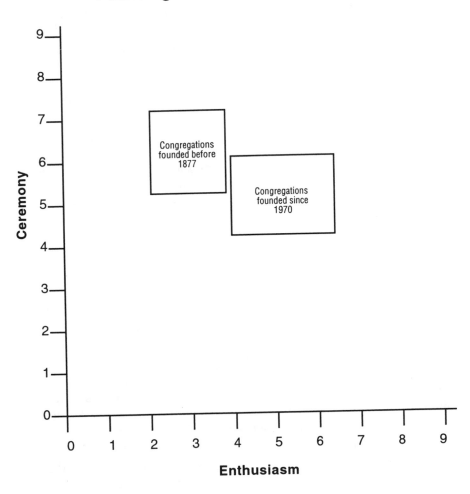

definitively discern the relative importance of each of these two possibilities.

There is another aspect to the relationship between a congregation's founding date and its worship style. A not uncommon kind of conflict in congregations occurs when a subset of the congregation wants to worship in a way that is more enthusiastic and/or less ceremonial than what might be the congregation's long-standing way of worshiping. People often are willing to fight over changes in worship, and if the more established and central members of a congregation favor maintaining the less enthusiastic, more ceremonial style, a likely result is that those who want a different style will break off and begin a new congregation with worship practices more to their liking. If this is a common source of congregational conflict and schism, it would reinforce the relationship shown in figure 9: newer congregations will display worship practices that are more enthusiastic and less ceremonial than the older congregations from which they broke.

Paid Staff

Congregations with at least one paid staff member—either full-time or part-time—exhibit both more ceremony and more enthusiasm than do congregations with no paid staff. This relationship is not shown in a figure because it is evident only when controlling for other congregational characteristics, such as size and denomination. Still, it is important to note that NCS results suggest that congregations with paid staff are able to mount worship services that have more elements on both of these important dimensions of worship. This probably is another reflection of the fact, touched on in the discussion about congregational size, that it takes human and material resources to produce worship services. Although a group of people certainly can construct meaningful worship events without the help of a specialist, it seems that a paid staff person, usually a clergyperson, adds something to worship. Such a person, whatever other duties he or she might have, probably is responsible for putting together worship services. Having such a person on board increases both the level of ceremony and the level of enthusiasm in worship, perhaps because a paid person has the time and perhaps the expertise to develop and introduce additional elements to a congregation's worship.

BOX 5

Worship and Resources

The issue of resources has come up several times in this report. Collective worship requires both human and material resources—a space to be in, people with time to prepare for the event, people with expertise in certain kinds of worship elements, well-maintained musical instruments and other items, and so on. NCS data suggest that there is a relationship between the type of worship that can be achieved and the level of resources available for achieving it.

It could be informative to list all the resources your congregation devotes to worship and then ponder the relationship between these resources and what worship is like in your congregation. How much of your physical facility is dedicated to worship space? What percentage of paid staff time is spent preparing for and leading worship? How many hours of volunteer time go into worship? How much money is spent to enhance worship beyond what regular staff and volunteers can do? If you could devote additional resources—either material or human—to worship, what would you add or change? If you were faced with the need to reduce the current level of resources—either material or human—devoted to worship, what would you subtract or change?

CONCLUSION

The preceding chapters of this report explored the relationship between worship style and denomination, racial composition, age composition, income level, region, size, founding date, and paid staff. A disadvantage of treating these factors one at a time is that it is difficult to discern the relative importance of each. Is each of these variables equally strongly related to worship styles, or are some more strongly related than others? Additional, more complex, analyses permit an answer to this question. To oversimplify, although each of these variables has some independent effect on worship, the order of importance of these variables in their effect on a congregation's worship style is roughly as follows: size, race, denomination, founding date, age composition, presence of paid staff, income level, and region.

Some of these factors are much more important for one dimension of worship than for the other. As described above, for example, size matters much more for the level of ceremony in worship than for the level of enthusiasm; the opposite is true for race. In general, though, we can expect that congregations experiencing change in their size or their ethnic composition, for example, will face more immediate and profound challenges to their worship practices than will congregations experiencing change in the income level or age composition of their people. This is not to say that change in income level or age structure is likely to be irrelevant for worship; it is merely to suggest that these types of changes are likely to pose less dramatic and deep challenges for worship than will changes in size or ethnic composition.

Just as the nine elements in each scale should not be construed as the only elements relevant to ceremony or enthusiasm–a point made in box 1– these two dimensions are not the only dimensions on which worship events

BOX 6

What Factors Affect Worship—
or Conflict over Worship—
in Your Congregation?

We have seen that, overall, worship style can be influenced by a congregation's size, racial composition, denomination, founding date, age composition, presence of paid staff, income level, and regional location. How any of these factors might affect worship—or conflict over worship—in a specific congregation is impossible to say from the outside. Here are some questions that might help you to make connections between the patterns described in this report and what happens in your congregation. Thinking about them might help you to understand better what your congregation currently is experiencing in its worship life.

1. Of the various factors discussed in this report, which would you say most influences the practice of worship in your congregation?
2. What additional factors that have not been discussed here are important in your case?
3. If your congregation is experiencing conflict over worship, is it because one or another of these factors is changing? If so, what factors are involved?
4. Is your congregation growing or declining in ways that have consequences for worship? What do you believe the consequences might be?
5. Are you experiencing change in the ethnic, age, or social-class composition of your congregation in ways that affect worship? Again, what do you believe the consequences might be?
6. Does your congregation include newcomers from other parts of the country or other denominations who bring expectations regarding worship different from those of longtime members? How has your congregation responded to these expectations?
7. Have you experienced recent expansion or contraction in staff size or in other resources connected to worship? If so, how has your congregation's worship changed as a result?

might vary. Worship might profitably be analyzed along a music dimension, for example, that might be defined in terms of all the different sorts of musical elements that a worship service might include. Or we might construct a participation dimension defined in terms of all the ways–formal or informal–that people other than the official worship leaders speak, sing, or participate bodily in the worship service by kneeling or standing or coming to the front of the worship space. The point here is that although ceremony and enthusiasm were emphasized in this report as two important dimensions of worship, other dimensions also could be considered.

"Is" does not imply "ought," and neither this report nor NCS data can tell anyone how they should worship. There might be excellent and legitimate reasons, for example, to keep worship on the low end of the enthusiasm scale even if that congregation has many African Americans or young people in it. Similarly, there may be excellent reasons for a congregation to move far from its denomination's center of gravity when it comes to worship. National Congregations Study data, however, can facilitate in a variety of ways systematic comparison between the worship of a particular congregation and the average worship in congregations that are similar to that congregation.

This report is offered in the hope that knowledge about where a congregation fits within a larger map of worship practices can help congregations to think about their worship in a new way by posing questions such as these: Why are we higher or lower in ceremony or enthusiasm than the average congregation in our denomination? Why are we higher or lower in ceremony or enthusiasm than the average congregation with similar percentages of young people, or African Americans, or low-income people? Why are we higher or lower in ceremony or enthusiasm than the average congregation of similar size? In light of each of these comparisons, is our worship where we want it to be? If our worship is near the average for congregations like ours, do we want to be so typical? This report advocates no particular answer to any of these questions. It does, however, advocate asking these questions and using NCS data to spark informed conversation about possible answers.

About the National Congregations Study

The organizations to which a representative sample of individuals belong constitute a representative sample of organizations. It is therefore possible to generate a representative sample of organizations even in the absence of a comprehensive list of those organizations. This fact is important because there is no comprehensive list of religious congregations in the United States. Denominational lists vary in quality and completeness and would not in any case include the approximately 18% of congregations that are not associated with any denomination. Telephone books miss as many as 15% of the smallest and least established congregations.

The National Congregations Study bypassed these sampling problems by starting with a random sample of individuals–respondents to the General Social Survey (GSS), a national survey of English-speaking noninstitutionalized adults conducted almost annually by the National Opinion Research Center at the University of Chicago. Each GSS respondent who attended religious services was asked the name and location of his or her congregation. These congregations then became the NCS sample.

In addition to the worship material discussed in this report, the NCS contains information about a wide range of congregational features. These data address the following questions, among others: To what extent do congregations engage in political activity? What proportion distribute voter guides? What proportion organize demonstrations, lobby elected officials, or have small groups devoted to political discussion? How much social service activity do congregations conduct? What percentage are interested in pursuing government funds to support their social service activity? How connected are congregations to other organizations in their communities? What kinds of small groups do congregations have? What constituencies do they mainly serve? How common (or uncommon) are ethnically mixed congregations? What are the features of such congregations? What are the characteristics of clergy in American congregations? How many congregations are led by women? By part-time leaders? By people without higher education? What percentage of congregations have substantial numbers of new immigrants? How common is serious conflict in American congregations? These are only some of the questions NCS data can address. Future NCS reports will focus on these and other issues.

In general, the margin of error for percentages calculated using NCS data is plus-or-minus 3%. This means, for example, that, if in the NCS data 59% of congregations have fewer than 100 regular participants, we can be 95% confident that, in the full national population of U.S. congregations, between 56% and 62% have fewer than 100 regular participants. Readers interested in more detail about NCS methodology should see, "The National Congregations Study: Background, Methods, and Selected Results," by Mark Chaves, Mary Ellen Konieczny, Kraig Beyerlein, and Emily Barman, *Journal for the Scientific Study of Religion* 38, no. 4 (December 1999).